TWELVE POETS AT EDINBURGH PARK

NATIONAL GALLERIES OF SCOTLAND

EDINBURGH · 2005

Published by the Trustees of the National Galleries of Scotland to celebrate the gift of twelve portrait busts to the Scottish National Portrait Gallery and to accompany the exhibition *Twelve Poets*, being held at the gallery from 25 February to 24 April 2005.

Poems © the poets or their estates

Biographical notes on the poets © Scottish Poetry Library

Biographical notes on the sculptors © Trustees of the National Galleries of Scotland

Herms and Edinburgh Park texts © Ian Wall

Illustrations © Paul Zanre Photography

Designed by Dalrymple

Typeset in Cycles and Arepo

Printed in Poland by Druk Intro

ISBN 1 903278 67 8

Preface

The decision by New Edinburgh Ltd to commission portrait busts of twelve of Scotland's leading poets, to be executed by a group of sculptors working in Scotland today, was an inspired and an inspiring initiative. We have been particularly pleased to see this project develop from its first proposal to its final fruition – the unveiling of the last group of so-called 'herms' (four were done each year for three years until all twelve were in place) in the summer of 2004. Or at least, that was what we took to be the conclusion. In fact, to our great pleasure, on that occasion we were told by Ian Wall, whose vision and dedication has been at the heart of this project, that he wished the Scottish National Portrait Gallery to accept the gift of a second cast of each of the portraits. We have been pleased to accept this gift, and we in turn wish to extend the project further by ensuring that as many people in Scotland, in as many different places, will be able to see the exhibition of the twelve poets. In this way we help to celebrate not only an impressive act of patronage of the arts in Scotland, but further the aims of Ian Wall and his associates to celebrate Scotland's rich literary heritage. In doing so we hope to extend the pleasure and enrichment of our lives that is the essence of poetry.

SIR TIMOTHY CLIFFORD
Director-General, National Galleries of Scotland

JAMES HOLLOWAY
Director, Scottish National Portrait Gallery

Herms

Our interest in poetry in Edinburgh Park began with the display of regularly changing poems in our bus shelters to provide enjoyment to passengers and passers-by.

Building upon the idea of poetry within the park and stimulated by the example of the architect Josef Plecznik in Ljubljana, we decided to enrich the park at the heart of Edinburgh Park with twelve herms of twentieth-century Scottish poets.

The centrepiece of the design for the park, by Richard Meier & Partners, is the central park with three lochans designed by Ian White Associates. Two of these have been built to date, with their western edges straight and hard, backed with a line of horse chestnuts at four metre centres. This rhythm of trees was determined by the eight-metre cartesian grid which controls almost all buildings and features of the park; working within this grid, we calculated that four herms per lochan would stimulate interest without being too rich and overpowering; thus with three lochans and four per lochan, twelve becomes the number.

In the same manner that the grid provides a discipline and a coherence for the park, it was felt the subjects of the herms should be restricted and thus, rather than considering all Scottish poetry, we determined to limit ourselves to the twentieth century though, given the quality and richness of Scottish poetry in that century, the most difficult problem was the restriction to twelve.

As to why these twelve? There is no formal 'rhyme or reason' particularly as we took a wide view of the nature of poets' contribution to Scottish life; the discussions about who should be in and out were stimulating and enjoyable and any one of us would want to bring in other poets, but no justification for the twelve will be given here.

No such group could be considered definitive and this leads to one of our other objectives, which was to provide a series of small commissions for Scottish sculptors. Such work is the bread and butter of artistic life and arguably more important than the occasional great set pieces. Our main aim was to provide pleasure and interest to the people working in and visiting Edinburgh Park but, in addition to that, if others are encouraged to commission sculptures of the poets we have missed, we will be very pleased for the sculptors and the poets.

IAN WALL
Director, New Edinburgh Ltd

Edinburgh Park

Other sculptures at South Gyle

EDINBURGH PARK

Epitaph for the Elm Tim Stead
Questor Keith McCarter

GYLE SHOPPING CENTRE

Fossil Tree Bill Scott
Veil Jake Kempsall
Stacked Spares Marion Smith
Concrete Jungle Alan Watson
Figure in a Landscape Sylvia Stewart
Strange Attractor Alistair White
Two Constellations for a Column
Ian Hamilton Finlay

ROYAL BANK OF SCOTLAND,
REDHEUGHS ROAD

Wealth of Nations Eduardo Paolozzi
Primavera Peter Maine

17 SOUTH GYLE CRESCENT

Burdz do sit (six sculptures)
Shona Kinloch

Edinburgh Park is a large, modern office park on the west side of Edinburgh with access from South Gyle Broadway. The overall approach to the design was, and is, to create a place which will provide pleasure to those who work in and visit it. This manifests itself in the quality of the architecture and landscape and in the range of commercial and social facilities present.

The herms are not the first sculptures in the park – other works include *Questor* by Keith McCarter and *Epitaph for the Elm* by Tim Stead, with its title stone by Ian Hamilton Finlay; nor are the herms the only manifestation of poetry within the park. The bus shelters, the first two by Reiach and Hall and the third by Linda Tolmie, have a regular changing programme of poetry within or beside the shelters, all of which adds to the richness of the environment.

The British Council of Offices described Edinburgh Park as '… one of the best business parks in Europe'; this is an accolade, but also a high standard which we intend to continue to match.

It would not have been possible for Edinburgh Park to have carried out this programme without the immense help of Robyn Marsack and the Scottish Poetry Library. This great resource run by a committed, skilled and helpful staff is available to all at Crichton's Close, a few steps off the Royal Mile.

Douglas Dunn by Michael Snowden

Born in Inchinnan, Renfrewshire, in 1942, Dunn trained as a librarian and worked in England and the USA. Since 1991 he has been professor in the School of English at the University of St Andrews. Also a short-story writer and noted anthologist, Dunn has won many awards for his poetry. His twelve collections include *St Kilda's Parliament* (1981), *Elegies* (1985), and *New Selected Poems* (2003). The conversational tone that characterises much of his work is underpinned by great technical accomplishment. Dunn is able to embed individual stories within their larger political and historical contexts, his strong sense of social justice always apparent. Honesty, fidelity to imaginative truth, and an eye for the telling detail mark his poetry as he meditates on Scottish and other landscapes, on private and public histories. Pricked by grief and memory, Dunn has produced his generation's most impressive body of poetry.

Further Reading
New Selected Poems 1964–2000 (Faber & Faber, 2003)
ISBN 0571215270
The Year's Afternoon (Faber & Faber, 2000)
ISBN 0571204279

EMPTY WARDROBES

I sat in a dress shop, trying to look
As dapper as a young ambassador
Or someone who'd impressed me in a book,
A literary rake or movie star.

Clothes are a way of exercising love,
False? A little. And did she like it? Yes.
Days, days, romantic as Rachmaninov,
A ploy of style, and now not comfortless.

She walked out from the changing-room in brown,
A pretty smock with its embroidered fruit;
Dress after dress, a lady-like red gown
In which she flounced, a smart career-girl's suit.

The dress she chose was green. She found it in
Our clothes-filled cabin trunk. The pot-pourri,
In muslin bags, was full of where and when,
I turn that scent like a memorial key.

But there's that day in Paris, that I regret,
When I said No, franc-less and husbandly,
She browsed through hangers in the Lafayette,
And that comes back tonight, to trouble me.

Now there is grief the couturier, and grief
The needlewoman mourning with her hands,
And grief the scattered finery of life,
The clothes she gave as keepsakes to her friends.

From *Elegies* published by Faber & Faber 1985

W. S. Graham by Anthony Morrow

Greenock-born (William) Sydney Graham (1918–1986) lived near water for most of his life, spending the latter half in Cornwall. He completed an apprenticeship in engineering and later attended Newbattle Abbey College, but after the war scraped a living from his writing. His poetry was admired and published by T. S. Eliot, notable collections being *The Nightfishing* (1955) and *Implements in their Places* (1977). A need to communicate is one of his chief themes, along with the obdurate strangeness of language itself as the medium for communication: 'the inadequacy / Of the living, animal language drives / Us all to metaphor'. Graham's originality, his enlivening and disturbing use of words, was both radical and oddly charming, like the man himself. His poems – often intimate in tone – and his voice retained their Scottish timbre. The integrity of his endeavour and the unmistakable music of his work make him one of the most valuable twentieth-century poets.

Further Reading
New Collected Poems, edited by Matthew Francis (Faber & Faber, 2004)
ISBN 0571210155
Selected Poems (Faber & Faber, 1996)
ISBN 0571176593

FROM 'THE DARK DIALOGUES'

I hear the blind horn
Mourning from the firth.
The big wind blows
Over the shore of my child
Hood in the off-season.
The small wind remurmurs
The fathering tenement
And a boy I knew running
The hide and seeking streets.
Or do these winds
In their forces blow
Between the words only?

I am the shell held
To Time's ear and you
May hear the lonely leagues
Of the kittiwake and the fulmar.

From *New Collected Poems*
published by Faber & Faber 2004

Hamish Henderson by Anthony Morrow

Born in Perthshire in 1919, Henderson finished his schooling in England and volunteered for service in 1939. Commissioned as an intelligence officer, he served in North Africa, Italy and Austria, at the same time collecting material for his first book, *Ballads of World War II, in Five Languages*. Politics, poetry and folksong were inseparable in his life, and the focus of his pioneering work in the School of Scottish Studies in Edinburgh. He was the leader of the Folksong Revival in Scotland, his own memorable songs including the 'The Freedom Come-All-Ye', written in Perthshire Scots. A talented linguist and translator, and poet of considerable achievement – notably in *Elegies for the Dead in Cyrenaica* – he loved the communal values of song. He envisaged a Scotland that was free, fraternal and joyful, and by the time of his death in 2002 had conveyed his vision to thousands.

Further Reading
Collected Poems and Song, edited by Raymond Ross (Curly Snake Publishing, 2000)
ISBN 1902141016

THE FREEDOM COME-ALL-YE

Roch the wind in the clear day's dawin
  Blaws the cloods heelster-gowdie ow'r the bay,
But there's mair not a roch wind blawin
  Through the great glen o' the warld the day.
It's a thocht that will gar oor rottans
  – A'they rogues that gang gallus, fresh and gay –
Tak the road, and seek ither loanins
  For their ill ploys, tae sport and play.

Nae mair will the bonnie callants
  Mairch tae war when oor braggarts crousely craw,
Nor wee weans frae pit-heid and clachan
  Mourn the ships sailin' doon the Broomielaw.
Broken families in lands we've herriet,
  Will curse Scotland the Brave nae mair, nae mair;
Black and white, ane till ither mairriet,
  Mak the vile barracks o' their maisters bare.

So come all ye at hame wi' Freedom,
  Never heed whit the hoodies croak for doom.
In your hoose a' the bairns o' Adam
  Can find breid, barley-bree and painted room.
When MacLean meets wi's freens in Springburn
  A' the roses and geans will turn tae bloom,
And a black boy frae yont Nyanga
  Dings the fell gallows o' the burghers doon.

From *Collected Poems and Songs*
published by Curly Snake Publishing 2000

Jackie Kay by Michael Snowden

Born in 1961 of a Scottish mother and Nigerian father, Jackie Kay explored her own situation as the adopted child of white Scottish parents in her first collection of poems, *The Adoption Papers* (1991). First performed on radio, this award-winning work brought a new and hugely attractive voice to a wide audience. Kay has since published two more collections, an acclaimed novel, *Trumpet* (1998), plays and short stories, all character-ised by a generous humanity. Her understanding of the deeply familiar experiences of daughters, mothers, lovers is filtered through the sensibility of an outsider. She is alert to the register of languages, and to the power of language to make people feel at home or unwelcome. Her protagonists often move through contested spaces, at odds with their surroundings or their histories, but their strength, their humour and their capacity for love are sources of the joy that also permeates her work.

Further Reading

Off Colour (Bloodaxe Books, 1998)
ISBN 1852244208

Modern Scottish Women Poets, edited by Dorothy McMillan and Michel Byrne (Canongate Books, 2003)
ISBN 184195294X

LIFE MASK (FOR JULIA DARLING)

When the senses come back in the morning,
The nose is a mouth full of spring;
The mouth is an earful of birdsong;
The eyes are lips on the camomile lawn;
The ear is an eye of calm blue sky.

When the broken heart begins to mend,
The heart is a bird with a tender wing
The tears are pear blossom blossoming
The shaken love grows green shining leaves.
The throat doesn't close, it is opening

Like a long necked swan in the morning,
Like the sea and the river meeting,
Like the huge heron's soaring wings:
I sat up with my pale face in my hands
And all of a sudden it was spring.

Written to accompany the herm

JACKIE KAY

Life Mask (for Julia Darling)

When the senses come back in the morning,
The nose is a mouth full of spring;
The mouth is an earful of birdsong;
The eyes are lips on the camomile lawn;
The ear is an eye of calm blue sky.

When the broken heart begins to mend,
The heart is a bird with a tender wing,
The tears are pear blossom blossoming,
The shaken love grows green shining leaves,
The throat doesn't close, it is opening.

Like a long necked swan in the morning,
Like the sea and the river meeting,
Like the huge heron's soaring wings,
... with my pale face in my hands
... den it was spring.

Tom Leonard by Alex Main

Born in Glasgow in 1944, Tom Leonard has made the city's voices heard throughout Scotland, and beyond. 'If you don't treat language seriously, you don't treat people seriously': the consequences of this statement are apparent in all of his work, notably that involving the transcription of Glasgow speech. Leonard's political, aesthetic and linguistic concerns are inextricable. His poetry contrasts different voices, social classes, emotional registers, philosophies. It is often funny but fiercely so. He has been writer-in-residence in libraries and universities, and in the anthology *Radical Renfrew*, he trawled the Paisley archives to reconstruct the region's literary past from the French Revolution to the First World War. His own work has been collected in *Intimate Voices* (1984) and *Reports from the Present* (1995), powerfully presenting what Edwin Morgan has called 'the authenticities and indignations which have moved him to act and write'.

Further Reading

Intimate Voices: Poems 1965–1983 (Etruscan Books, 2004)
ISBN 1901538404

access to the silence: poems and posters 1984–2004 (Etruscan Books, 2004)
ISBN 1901538478

PROEM

who are we, trapped in our ways
                    of dying towards the fact
of only once having been, together

or separate in our own being
                    but never wholly separate, only a part
of the time we live in, and with others occupy

From *Intimate Voices*
published by Etruscan Books 2004

Tom Leonard

Born in Glasgow in 1944, Tom Leonard has
made the city's voices heard throughout
Scotland, and beyond. *"If you don't treat
language seriously, you don't treat people
seriously"*: the consequences of this
statement are apparent in all of his work,
notably that involving the transcription of
Glasgow speech. Leonard's political,
aesthetic and linguistic concerns are
inextricable. His poetry contrasts different
voices, social classes, emotional registers,
philosophies. It is often funny but fiercely
so. He has been writer-in-resid...

Liz Lochhead by Vincent Butler

Born in Motherwell in 1947 and trained at the Glasgow School of Art, Lochhead published her first collection, *Memo for Spring*, in 1971, with immediate success. In the predominantly male domain of Scottish poetry, here was a fresh voice, of women speaking to women, speaking for women. Her poems, prose and drama escape the boundaries of each genre, using the speech she hears around her, poignant and humorous. Questioning assumptions about female and Scottish identity, Lochhead has forged powerful and personal theatrical pieces. *Mary Queen of Scots Got Her Head Chopped Off* and her translation of *Tartuffe* are written in Scots, her poems in Scots and English: 'To tell the stories was her work.' These stories, grounded in recognisable lives, are told with tenderness and irony. Lochhead draws on ballad and fairy-tale to give them a deeper life, often a darker one. She has been a liberating, inspiring literary presence.

Further Reading

The Colour of Black and White: Poems 1984 – 2003 (Polygon, 2003)
ISBN 0954407520

Dreaming Frankenstein and Collected Poems 1967 – 1984 (new edition) (Polygon, 2003)
ISBN 0954407512

True Confessions and New Clichés (new edition) (Polygon, 2003)
ISBN 0954407539

SORTING THROUGH

The moment she died, my mother's dance
dresses turned from the colours they really were
to the colours I imagine them to be.
I can feel the weight of bumptoed silver shoes
swinging from their anklestraps as she swaggers up
the path towards *her* dad, light-headed
from airman's kisses. Here, at what I'll have to learn
to call *my father's house*, yes every
ragbag scrap of duster prints her even more vivid
than an Ilford snapshot on some seafront
in a white cardigan and that exact frock.
Old lipsticks. Liquid stockings.
Labels like *Harella*, *Gor-ray* and *Berketex*.
As I manhandle whole outfits into binbags for Oxfam
every mote in my eye is a utility mark
and this is useful:
the sadness of dispossessed dresses,
the decency of good coats roundshouldered
in the darkness of wardrobes,
the gravitas of lapels,
the invisible danders of skin fizzing off from them
like all that life that will not neatly end.

From *The Colour of Black & White: Poems 1984–2003*
published by Polygon 2003

16

Norman MacCaig by David Annand

Born in Edinburgh, Norman MacCaig (1910–1996) studied classics at the University of Edinburgh and was a schoolteacher for much of his life. He was a prolific writer of poetry marked by elegance, wit and sharp insight. The landscapes of his work – also the settings for his distinctive character studies – are those of Edinburgh and of Assynt in the Highlands, where he spent his summers. The 'unemphatic marvels' of the natural world were a particular province, and its small inhabitants feature in some of his most admired poems. Everything was seen afresh, and the poet was openly conscious of his act of seeing, of the search to find language adequate to his perceptions. His range of subjects and laconic yet benign presentation drew crowds to his readings, finding him an audience even among those resistant to poetry. This 'Zen Calvinist', as he described himself, was one of Scotland's finest twentieth-century writers.

Further Reading
Collected Poems (Chatto & Windus, 1990)
The Poems of Norman MacCaig (Polygon, 2005)

NOTATIONS OF TEN SUMMER MINUTES

A boy skips flat stones out to sea – each does fine
till a small wave meets it head on and swallows it.
The boy will do the same.

The schoolmaster stands looking out of the window
with one Latin eye and one Greek one.
A boat rounds the point in Gaelic.

Out of the shop comes a stream
of Omo, Weetabix, BiSoDol tablets and a man
with a pocket shaped like a whisky bottle.

Lord V. walks by with the village in his pocket.
Angus walks by
spending the village into the air.

A melodeon is wheezing a clear-throated jig
on the deck of the *Arcadia*. On the shore hills Pan
cocks a hairy ear; and falls asleep again.

The ten minutes are up, except they aren't.
I leave the village, except I don't.
The jig fades to silence, except it doesn't.

From *The Poems of Norman MacCaig*
to be published by Polygon 2005

Hugh MacDiarmid by Anthony Morrow

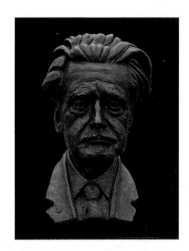

Hugh MacDiarmid (Christopher Murray Grieve) was born in Langholm in 1892 and died in Biggar in 1978. He worked as a journalist in Scotland and Wales, serving in the RAMC during the First World War. He adopted the literary name 'Hugh MacDiarmid', and the writing career that he himself described as 'volcanic activity' got underway in the 1920s. His output in poetry and prose was prodigious and always controversial. He wrote poems in Scots, mixing the literary with the vernacular. *A Drunk Man Looks at the Thistle* (1926) is the most ambitious expression of his critical nationalism and fervent internationalism. MacDiarmid galvanised the Scottish Renaissance movement. A member of the Communist Party and a founding member of the National Party of Scotland, he was expelled from and rejoined both. His later philosophical poetry (in English) shows his vigorous intellect and engagement with scientific thought. MacDiarmid is recognised as the towering Scottish literary figure of the twentieth century.

Further Reading

Selected Poems, edited by Alan Riach and Michael Grieve (Fyfield Books, 2004)
ISBN 185754756X

The Revolutionary Art of the Future: Rediscovered Poems, edited by John Manson, Dorian Grieve and Alan Riach (Carcanet / Scottish Poetry Library, 2003)
ISBN 1857547330

Complete Poems, Vols. 1 & 2, edited by Michael Grieve and W.R. Aitken (Carcanet, 1993 & 1994)
ISBN 185754014X / 185754062X

THE BONNIE BROUKIT BAIRN (FOR PEGGY)

Mars is braw in crammasy,
Venus in green silk goun,
The auld mune shak's her gowden feathers,
Their starry talk's a wheen o' blethers,
Nane for thee a thochtie sparin',
Earth, thou bonnie broukit bairn!
— *But greet, an' in your tears ye'll droun*
The haill clanjamfrie!

From *Complete Poems*, Vol. 1
published by Carcanet 1993

HUGH
MacDIARMID

Hugh MacDiarmid

Christopher Murray Grieve : born
Langholm, 1892; died Biggar, 1978. He
worked as a journalist in Scotland and
Wales, serving in the RAMC during the
First World War. He adopted the literary
name 'Hugh MacDiarmid', and the writing
career that he himself described as
'volcanic activity' got underway in the
1920's. His po...

Sorley MacLean by Bill Scott

Born in 1911 on the Isle of Raasay, Sorley MacLean grew up within a rich Gaelic culture, especially of song. Having studied English Literature at the University of Edinburgh in the 1930s, he fought in North Africa during the Second World War. He became head teacher at Plockton High School and was instrumental in preserving the teaching of Gaelic in Scottish schools. A highly influential figure at the heart of the Gaelic renaissance in Scotland, MacLean published his groundbreaking collection *Dàin do Eimhir* in 1943, passionate poems of love and politics. His work remained little-known outside Gaelic-speaking circles until the 1970s, when he came to the attention of a much wider public, and published his major collection *Reothairt is Contraigh/SpringTide and Neap Tide*. He received the Queen's Gold Medal for Poetry in 1990, and died in 1996, mourned as the greatest Gaelic poet of the century.

Further Reading

Dàin do Eimhir / Poems to Eimhir, edited by Christopher Whyte (Association for Scottish Literary Studies, 2002)
ISBN 0948877502

O Choille gu Bearradh / From Wood to Ridge: Collected Poems in Gaelic and in English Translation (new edition) (Carcanet / Birlinn, 1999)
ISBN 190310100X

CREAGAN BEAGA

Tha mi dol troimh Chreagan Beaga
anns an dorchadas liom fhìn
agus an rod air Camus Alba
´na shian air a´ mhol mhìn.

Tha ´n guilbirneach´s an fheadag
ag éigheach shìos mu ´n Chùil,
´s an earraidheas air Sgurr nan Gillean,
Blàbheinn, ´s a´ ghealach gun smùr.

Stràcadh na soillse air clàr mara
o Rubha na Fainge sìnte tuath,
agus an sruth an Caol na h-Airde
a´ ruith gu deas le lainnir luaith.

CREAGAN BEAGA

I am going through Creagan Beaga
in the darkness alone
and the surf on Camus Alba
is a sough on smooth shingle.

The curlew and the plover
are crying down about the Cuil;
and south-east of Sgurr nan Gillean,
Blaven, and the stainless moon.

The light levels the sea flatness
from Rubha na Fainge stretched north,
and the current in Caol na h-Airde
is running south with swift glitter.

From *O Choille gu Bearradh / From Wood to Ridge*
published by Carcanet / Birlinn 1999

Sorley MacLean/Somhairle MacGill-Eain

Born in 1911 on the Isle of Raasay, Sorley
MacLean grew up within a rich Gaelic
culture, especially of song. Having studied
English Literature at the University of
Edinburgh in the 1930's, he fought in North
Africa during the Second World War. He
became head teacher at Plockton High
School and was instrumental in preserving
the teaching of Gaelic in Scottish schools. A
highly influential figure at the heart of the
Gaelic renaissance in Scotl...

SORLEY
MacLEAN

Naomi Mitchison by Archie Forrest

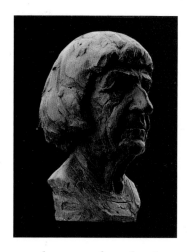

Born in Edinburgh in 1897, Naomi Haldane married the Labour politician G. Richard Mitchison and in 1937 they bought Carradale House in Kintyre, where she became deeply involved in local political life. Mitchison's first novels sprang from her interest in classical history and mythology, notably *The Corn King and the Spring Queen* (1931), while in the 1940s and 1950s Scottish themes dominated her writing. Her sense of the common human endeavour was also expressed in her affinity with the Bakgatha tribe of Botswana, which adopted her as their advisor and 'mother' in the 1960s. By the time of her death in 1999, she had published over seventy works. A storyteller in prose and poetry, she had a distinctive poetic voice, combining conversational ease with the strength of the ballad tradition. Daring, as a woman, to speak for her tribes, drawing on ancient collective memory while articulating the dilemmas and loyalties peculiar to certain places and times, Mitchison occupied a unique place in twentieth-century Scottish literature.

Further Reading

The Cleansing of the Knife and Other Poems (Canongate, 1978)
ISBN 0903937344

Modern Scottish Women Poets, edited by Dorothy McMillan and Michel Byrne (Canongate, 2003)
ISBN 184195294X

KINTYRE

I wake when the wind changes.
Beyond the dark Firth far,
Where the waves clap and the tides rustle
     and the herring are,
At the far side of the great Clyde the wind ranges.
I wake as it changes.

If snow flew or mist blew
East on the hills of Renfrew,
Here, Arran sheltered, we might never know,
Get no breath of sleet or hard snow,
Until across mountain ranges
The wind backs and changes.

Clear starlight as sleep takes me,
But a cloud creeps from the side.
My dream no more ranges
Through a universe at rest,
But quick through the window wide,
From Atlantic on the west
Or from east beyond the Clyde,
Leaps anxious into my breast.
I wake when the wind changes.

From *The Cleansing of the Knife*
published by Canongate 1978

Edwin Morgan by David Annand

On 16 February 2004 it was announced that the Scottish Executive had appointed Edwin Morgan as 'Scots Makar', in effect Scotland's poet laureate. He is the first to hold this post, created to recognize the achievement of Scottish poets throughout the centuries. Born in Glasgow in 1920, Morgan has lived in Glasgow all his life, except for service with the RAMC in the Middle East during the Second World War, and his poetry is grounded in the city. He retired from Glasgow University as titular Professor of English in 1980, serving as Glasgow's first Poet Laureate 1999–2002. The title of his 1973 collection, *From Glasgow to Saturn*, suggests the range of Morgan's subject matter. Endlessly curious, open-minded and humane, Morgan has experimented with the language of machines as well as translating brilliantly from a variety of European languages. He has translated plays into Scots, and written a trilogy on the life of Jesus, *AD*. His *Sonnets from Scotland* rank as one of the most important works of post-war literature, exploring the life, landscapes and potential of the country. Morgan's poetry is marked by inventiveness, acceptance of change and an exhilarating energy.

Further Reading

Love and a Life (Mariscat Press, 2003)
ISBN 094658835X

Cathures: New Poems 1997 – 2001 (Carcanet / Mariscat, 2002)
ISBN 1857546172

New Selected Poems (Carcanet, 2000)
ISBN 1857545950

A human head would never do
under the mists and rains or tugged
by ruthless winds or whipped with leaves
from raving trees. But who is he
in bronze, who is the moveless one?
The poet laughed, It isn't me.
It's nearly me, but I am free
to dodge the showers or revel in them,
to walk the alleys under the stars
or waken where the blackbirds are.
Some day my veins will turn to bronze
and I won't hear, or make, a song.
Then indeed I shall be my head
staring ahead, or so it seems,
but you may find me watching you,
dear traveller, or wheeling round
into your dreams.

Written to accompany the herm

Iain Crichton Smith by Michael Snowden

Born in Glasgow in 1928, Iain Crichton Smith was brought up on the island of Lewis; he died in Taynuilt in 1998. He spent most of his working life as a schoolteacher, in Clydebank then Oban. He wrote prose and poetry in both Gaelic and English. The long poem 'Am Faigh a Ghaidhlig Eas?/ Shall Gaelic Die?' meditates on the fate of that language and culture. Often a deeply troubled man, and a self-deprecating writer, he could move an audience to tears of laughter with his 'Murdo' stories. *Consider the Lilies*, about the Highland Clearances, is a classic novel, but he considered himself more naturally a poet. Crichton Smith wrote poems of lyrical candour and great human understanding, as well as poems that speculated on the course and meaning of human existence. He was a much-loved man and poet, and some of his poems in English and in Gaelic have become touchstones for Scottish literature.

Further Reading

A Country for Old Men, and, My Canadian Uncle (Carcanet, 2000)
ISBN 1857544749

The Leaf and the Marble (Carcanet, 1998)
ISBN 1857544005

Collected Poems (Carcanet, 1992; 1995)
ISBN 1857542452

THE EXILES
(translated from the author's own Gaelic)

The many ships that left our country
with white wings for Canada.
They are like handkerchiefs in our memories
and the brine like tears
and in their masts sailors singing
like birds on branches.
That sea of May running in such blue,
a moon at night, a sun at daytime,
and the moon like a yellow fruit,
like a plate on a wall
to which they raise their hands
like a silver magnet
with piercing rays
streaming into the heart.

From *Collected Poems*
published by Carcanet 1992

Iain Crichton Smith

Iain Crichton Smith : born Glasgow, 1928;
died Taynuilt, 1998. Brought up on the
island of Lewis, Crichton Smith spent most
of his working life as a schoolteacher, in
Clydebank then Oban. He wrote prose and
poetry in both Gaelic and English. The
long poem *Am Faigh a Ghaidhlig Eas?/
Shall Gaelic Die?* meditates on the fate of
that language and culture. Often a deeply
troubled man, and a self depreciating
writer, he could move an audience to tears
of laughter with his 'Murdo' stories.
Consider the Lilies, about the Highland
Clearances, is a classic novel, but he
considered himself more naturally a poet.
Crichton Smith wrote poems of lyrical
candour and great human understanding,
as well as poems that speculated on the
course and meaning of human existence.
He was a much-loved man and poet, and
some of his poems

IAIN
CRICHTON
SMITH

The Sculptors

David Annand

Annand was born in 1948. He trained at Duncan of Jordanstone College of Art Dundee and tutored there for two years. After teaching in secondary schools for fourteen years he became a full-time sculptor. He has been the recipient of numerous awards, including the Royal Scottish Academy's Latimer Award, Benno Schotz Award and Ireland Alloys Award. In 1986 he won the Scottish Development Agency Dundee Technology Park competition to make *Deer Leap*, for which he was awarded the Sir Otto Beit Medal by the Royal Society of British Sculptors in 1987. Since then, Annand has undertaken numerous public and private sculpture commissions, among them *Royal Stag* for Baxters of Speyside (1993), the Tranent Massacre Memorial (1995), *Three Cranes in Flight* for the British High Commission in Hong Kong (1997), the Kelty Miners Memorial (1997) and the Robert Fergusson Memorial for Edinburgh (2004).

EDWIN MORGAN

David Annand writes: 'In my file marked Edwin Morgan and Norman MacCaig is a typewritten copy of Edwin Morgan's poem (see page 26) with a brief complimentary note signed, Eddie. The poem says more than I could ever about the sitter's relationship with the finished bronze and about Eddie's vitality and attitude to death. For the sculpture to be so endorsed is the greatest compliment I have ever had.'

NORMAN MACCAIG

On his portrait of Norman MacCaig Annand reflects: 'Having watched Norman MacCaig being interviewed by Magnus Magnusson, I was almost relieved to be working from photographs. He ripped him up and played with the little bits as he sooked contemplatively on his fags. When asked how long a poem took to write he replied, "two fags". His craggy features were a dream to work with and I felt it was like some of the rugged landscapes he loved. The photographs I was lent by his son were a treasure and should be a part of our national archive. I have a strong association with trying to incorporate poetry into my sculpture. The portraits are a different and demanding exercise in draughtsmanship and an attempt to empathise with the character whilst holding on to a likeness. In retrospect I would have loved to meet MacCaig and I think he would have enjoyed the process of posing. As a teacher he had a bit of the thespian about him. The sculpture should really have a fag in its gob. It's denuded without it.'

Vincent Butler

Butler was born in Manchester in 1933, and during the fifties trained at Manchester College of Art, Edinburgh College of Art and at the Academy of Fine Art in Milan. After almost a decade resident in Italy and later in Nigeria, he opened his studio in Edinburgh and has worked there ever since. Until 1989 he was a tutor at Edinburgh College of Art, specialising in modelling and bronze casting. He was elected a member of the Royal Scottish Academy in 1977 and is also a member of the Royal Glasgow Institute of Fine Art. He has had numerous solo exhibitions and regularly contributes to the major art societies in Scotland. He is also a skilled stone-cutter and the author of a technical manual on methods of casting in bronze, published by A. & C. Black. Recent works include a bronze bust of HRH the Duke of Edinburgh, a bust of Stewart, Lord Sutherland as Principal of the University of Edinburgh, and an over-life-sized bronze group for a new waterfront development at Granton in Edinburgh. The Scottish National Portrait Gallery has a cast of the bust of the Duke of Edinburgh, a bronze bust of the poet Helen Cruikshank, a bust of Cardinal Gray and a head of the sculptor Benno Schotz.

LIZ LOCHHEAD

This portrait, which is a little larger than life, was modelled in the sculptor's Stockbridge workshop in the relatively short time of four sittings with Liz Lochhead. The sculptor first made a plaster cast from the original clay model and from that produced two wax copies; from one of these a bronze was struck by Powderhall foundry, for Edinburgh Park.

Archie Forrest

Forrest was born in Glasgow in 1950. From 1969 to 1973 he trained at Glasgow School of Art where he worked as a tutor from 1978 to 1985. After teaching at Dumbartonshire schools between 1974 and 1985, he became a full-time artist. In 1988 he became member of the Royal Glasgow Institute of Fine Arts. Acclaimed as both a painter and a sculptor, he has twice been awarded the prestigious Royal Glasgow Institute's Benno Schotz Sculpture Award. Forrest has had numerous group and solo exhibitions and his work is in many private and public collections. Archie Forrest's sculpture in bronze of Donald Dewar, Scotland's First Minister after devolution in 1999, is in the Scottish National Portrait Gallery.

NAOMI MITCHISON

Forrest is another sculptor whose commission from Edinburgh Park entailed the additional challenge of having to make a posthumous portrait. Though free to choose at which stage of life he would depict her, he chose to represent not the young Naomi Mitchison, at the age when she was so strikingly portrayed by the artist Wyndham Lewis, but to represent her in old age. The sculptor has faithfully inscribed the network of lines that are to be seen in photographs of Mitchison in her nineties – and in doing so has made not just an uncompromising likeness but also an expression of her strength of character. It is a portrayal of a remarkable intellect.

Alex Main

Main was born in Edinburgh 1940. He was trained at Loughborough College of Art and Goldsmiths' and became an art teacher. Main now lives and works in the Highlands and regularly exhibits at Browns Gallery in Tain. He has exhibited at the Royal Scottish Academy and the Scottish National Portrait Gallery and is a regular contributor to the London and Glasgow Art Fairs. His work has featured in the Morrison Portrait Competition. Commissions include the Neil Gunn Memorial, Dunbeath. A bronze 'Head of John the Baptist' is in a private collection in Rome. Portraits by Main of the poets Norman McCaig and George Mackay Brown are in the collection of the Scottish National Portrait Gallery.

TOM LEONARD

Main writes that: 'A portrait commission has to satisfy the commissioners, the sitter, and the artist. The commissioners are paying, so they hope to get what they want; the sitter wants a likeness, and the artist is concerned with his integrity. Producing a portrait is a balancing act between these three,' writes Alex Main. This commission was particularly challenging for Main because his usual practice is to model from the life, during the course of several sittings. He continues: 'It was unfortunate that because of illness Tom was unable to come to the studio for sittings and so I had to work from photographs. Photography is devoid of movement, and doesn't allow for the play of light and shadow that I feel to be necessary, as, having no colour, I depend on highlights and hollows to animate the work and give it "life"'. In the end, however, and despite this difficulty, Main was satisfied with the final result both as a portrait and a sculpture.

Anthony Morrow

After working as an engineer for Strathclyde Fire Service for thirteen years, Anthony Morrow entered Duncan of Jordanstone College of Art, Dundee, as a mature student, and in 1988 was awarded the Mitchell Prize for Best First Year Student. He has subsequently taught sculpture and life drawing at the college. As well as public and private commissions, Morrow has undertaken restoration work, notably at St Magnus Cathedral on Orkney. His commissions include the restoration and casting in bronze of the Peter Pan monument to James Barrie at Kirriemuir. His works have been exhibited extensively and are in private collections in Australia, America and the UK. In 1998 he formed 'Jordanstone Sculptors' with his partner, the painter Suzi Paterson.

HUGH MACDIARMID

The first portrait commissioned from Morrow for Edinburgh Park was the herm of Hugh MacDiarmid . This was also the first of three posthumous portraits. Morrow's working method was to do extensive reading and research into the sitters as well as look at as many visual presentations of them, including paintings and photographs, as possible. In the case of MacDiarmid, he opted to portray the poet at his most immediately recognisable – the characteristic set jaw, gimlet eyes and 'wings' of wiry hair. He had been very attracted, however, by a photograph of the younger MacDiarmid, more open-faced and with hair cropped close to his head. When asked to make a second version of the herm for the Scottish National Portrait Gallery, he seized the opportunity to rework his portrait of MacDiarmid and to 'push it further' in sculptural terms.

W.S. GRAHAM

Morrow's research for his portrait of W.S. Graham involved looking at a group of photographs of the poet taken in the 1950s aged about forty. He was particularly intrigued by one that seemed to have caught him in a moment of introspection with a pensive, even anxious expression. It stood out among other photographs showing him as a confident, sociable man at ease with himself and others. It was this hint of a shadow of self-doubt that Morrow wanted to convey. The romantic mood of the piece is enhanced by the exaggerated wave of the poet's hair. Morrow also wanted this to contain a reference to Graham's abiding love of the sea.

HAMISH HENDERSON

Morrow was particularly pleased to be given the commission to make the portrait of Hamish Henderson. He had had the opportunity to make a portrait of Henderson fourteen years earlier, but the planned sittings had never taken place. The making of the posthumous portrait was both from photographic records and the sculptor's own memories of Henderson. In the second version, which has been given to the Scottish National Portrait Gallery, Morrow has reworked the portrait showing Henderson wearing his characteristic hat and scarf.

Bill Scott

Scott was born in Moniaive in 1935. He trained at Edinburgh College of Art and the Ecole des Beaux Arts in Paris. He taught at ECA and eventually became head of sculpture from 1990 to 1997. In 1994 he was appointed professor of the Faculty of Art and Design, at Heriot Watt University. In 1984 he was elected a member of the Royal Scottish Academy, and became secretary in 1998. He has also served as chairman of the board of Edinburgh Sculpture Workshop. Exhibiting widely both in the UK and abroad, Scott's commissions include works for the new Byre Theatre, St Andrews, Kentigern House, Glasgow, and a memorial to Sir Alec Douglas Home at Coldstream. His work is represented in numerous public collections.

SORLEY MACLEAN

Of his posthumous portrait of Sorley MacLean, Scott writes: 'The reference photographs included informal studies of MacLean at home or at public events or walking in his west highland landscape. Then there was a group of more formal studio portraits, some with a distant look and some studious. All showed him with a collar and tie. From his writing, his identity as a man of Raasay with all the depth of Gaelic tradition and culture is constant, and yet at the same time he was a European, concerned and connected with international politics and culture. His ethical conviction was clarified by a direct experience of war to which was added a strong measure of socialist idealism. On those occasions when I heard him read his own poetry aloud, everything changed. His delivery was never demonstrative, but the effect was impressive, caring and timeless, the tone set by a very evocative voice resonance and emphasised by quite hypnotic cadence.

Photographs give only a partial view, and a group of photographs only a series of bits and of course one very rarely gets information about the back of the head. In the first attempts there was something of a resolution to the form, but I became dissatisfied with the sense of the image being overscaled or over formal or something along those lines. Given my understanding of Sorley MacLean's character and interests, I remember that I wanted to depict a man with inner conviction and strength, not outward show. The dynamic of the head should be produced by the organisation of the forms of the whole head to create a quiet energy as well as a resemblance.'

Michael Snowden

Snowden was born in 1930. He was a student of sculpture with Karel Vogel at Camberwell School of Arts and Crafts, London from 1953 to 1962. From 1964 until 1995 he was a lecturer at Edinburgh College of Art. He is a professional member of the Society of Scottish Artists, an academician of the Royal Scottish Academy and in 1996 was elected to the Royal Glasgow Institute of Fine Arts. He has received many public commissions and taken part in solo and group exhibitions. His work is in the collections of the Arts Council of Great Britain and in private collections throughout the world.

IAIN CRICHTON SMITH

Snowden was apprehensive about making a posthumous portrait of Iain Crichton Smith. He writes: 'It was an enormous relief to discover from Donalda, his widow, that she had some video film of Iain. I made drawings of frozen moments from this to try to learn the forms so that they could be more easily grasped and realised in the clay. I was also able to see that even at his most serious moments Iain was a man in whom amusement was very close to the surface and he always seemed to have a twinkle in his eye. I felt that if I could represent something of this quality then I might have managed to represent something of the man. His writings gave me access to other aspects of his personality.'

JACKIE KAY

Snowden writes of this commission: 'Jackie was very excited about the prospect of having a portrait made of herself and curious about all of the stages in the process. When she learned that modelling the head in clay would be followed by a sequence of moulding and casting procedures, she wanted to know all about the methods and materials to be used… She was particularly excited by the experience of having her life mask made. At the first sitting she said that she would write a poem about her experience. About three weeks after her final visit to the studio I received a copy of not one but eight poems, each carrying the title of a stage in the process or of one of the materials used in the realisation of her portrait. The suite of poems is entitled *The Life Mask*.'

DOUGLAS DUNN

Snowden says in connection with this portrait: 'Working from life has been my lifetime's preoccupation as a sculptor. I have found that establishing an easygoing conversation with my models has always helped to put them at their ease. As a result, I am able to observe, almost surreptitiously, their passing moods and fleeting expressions whilst at the same time wrestling with the eternally perplexing problems of sculptural form. For Douglas, sitting for his portrait was not an entirely new experience and he asked no questions as to what I would do or why, seeming to know that his visits to my studio would require periods of intense and concentrated activity on my part. Nevertheless, we talked about many things and I discovered how seriously he took his teaching and all of his academic responsibilities.'

Scottish Poetry Library

'This house, this poem… this fresh hypothesis' is the line from a poem by Iain Crichton Smith engraved on glass in the Scottish Poetry Library. It is a purpose-built, award-winning building at Crichton's Close, a few steps off the Royal Mile down at the Holyrood end of Edinburgh. The building is a poem in itself, a light, airy and contemplative space. It contains about 30,000 volumes of poetry, mainly Scottish and mainly contemporary, but with a good admixture of other centuries and languages, together with periodicals, tapes, cds, volumes in Braille, and a small selection of books and cards for sale.

Anyone may use the library and borrow books – the catalogue is accessible through the website; and there are now eleven outlying collections housed in different venues in Scotland. The library also offers borrowing by post and inter-library loan so that readers from any part of the country can use its print as well as online resources. An education officer and an education outreach officer programme workshops and visits for schools and other institutions throughout Scotland.

The Edinburgh premises are a venue for readings and book launches, and the librarians are constantly answering inquiries about poems people want to trace and helping readers find poems for special occasions.

The Scottish Poetry Library is more than the elegant stone and wood that comprise its shell, however, more even than the books and people it houses: it exists to serve the art of poetry, and to celebrate and nurture the poetry of Scotland in particular.

SCOTTISH POETRY LIBRARY

5 Crichton's Close
Canongate

Edinburgh EH8 8DT
Telephone +44 (0)131 557 2876
Fax +44 (0)131 557 8393
Email inquiries@spl.org.uk

www.spl.org.uk